# THE RULERS OF OLDE ENGLAND

### In Verse or worse

### by

# IVOR D'OGGRELLE

*Colouring History Book from Clinical Press Ltd*

© Clinical Press Ltd. 2024

The right of Clinical Press Ltd. to be identified as the author and artist of this work has been asserted in accordance with the Copyright, Designs and Patents Act 1988.
All rights reserved. No part of this publication may be reproduced, stored in a retrieval system, or transmitted in any form or by any means, electronic, mechanical, photocopying, recording or otherwise, without prior permission from the copyright owner.
While the advice and information in this book is believed to be true and accurate at the time of going to press, neither the author, the editor, nor the publisher can accept legal responsibility for any errors of omissions that may be made. The publisher makes no warranty, express or implied, with respect to the material contained herein.

First published in the UK July 2024. A catalogue record for this book is available from the British Library
ISBN: 978-1-85457-136-6 The Rulers of Olde England by Ivor D'Ogrelle (paperback)
Published by: *Clinical Press Ltd.* Redland Green Farm, Redland, Bristol, BS6 7HF. *www.clinicalpress.co.uk*

# PREFACE

There are many histories of England and the author and illustrator of this small book has read some of them rather badly. Hence his grasp of reality is flawed. Why should Alfred the Great play in a jazz band? Jazz was not even invented when he was alive. How could Robin Hood do the things that they said he did? And where did his arrows go?

Ivor asks you not to take the verses too seriously since, if you do, you are in danger of damaging your mind.

*Horrible Histories* and *1066 and All That* are examples of this genre that do it much better than this offering. But if you liked them and you want to suffer here is the book for you.

History is a colourful subject so do have fun colouring in the various kings and queens of olde England.

Dates of the various reigns are given at the back of the book.

# KING ARTHUR*

## 6TH CENTURY

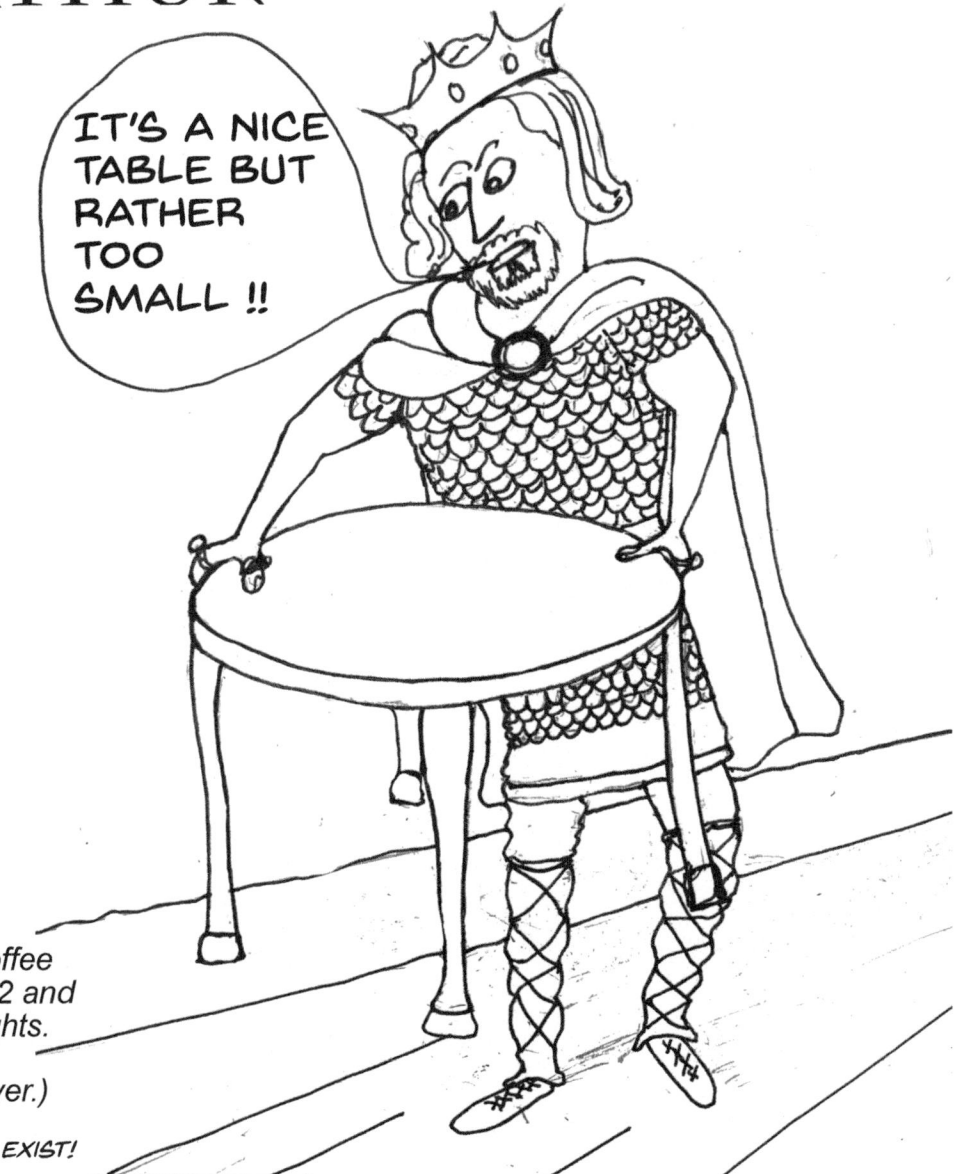

King Arthur is a legend
Perhaps a Romano-Briton
Who fought the Anglo-Saxons
And was finally smitten

He had a table
That his knights were able
To sit around
Once he was crowned

*It looks as if King Arthur's carpenter has accidentally invented the coffee table! Unfortunately London's first coffee house did not open until 1652 and Arthur needed a much bigger round table in order to seat all his knights.*

*(Why not colour Arthur as you like? You can also see him on the cover.)*

\* KING ARTHUR IS A DISPUTED LEGEND. SOME PEOPLE THINK THAT HE DID NOT EXIST!

# ANGLO-SAXONS AND DANES
# 860-1066

Alfred the Great
Burnt the cake*
But united much of olde Engla-land
I reckon today
If he had his way
He could lead a wild jazz band**

There was Egbert and Aethelwulf, Aethelbald and Aethelbert
Aethelred the First and Alfred the Great
Edward the Elder, Athelstan, Edmund, Edgar, Edward the Martyr
And Aethelred Unready who was always late

*That King Alfred burnt the cakes is also disputed (not everyone agrees)
**Jazz is a form of rhythmic, improvisational music first invented in the USA at the beginning of the 20th Century

*Interesting note: King Alfred's Cakes is a name given to a common, black, inedible fungus that lives on dead and decaying wood.*

# MORE ANGLO-SAXONS AND DANES

Yes, this brings us to Aethelred the Unready
Who fled from Sweyn the Dane
When Sweyn Forkbeard died
Our Aethelred cried
"I'll go back home again!"

Sweyn's son Canute
Thought Aethelred a brute
And gave him a right royal kicking
Aethelred's son Edmund II (The Ironside)
Made a pact with Canute then simply died
Leaving England ripe for the nicking

King Canute
Took the salute
From the Admiral of his navy
But the sea came up,*
Wet his butt
And he couldn't eat his gravy

*The story of Canute trying to turn back the tide is disbelieved by some historians and rather than showing pride he may have been doing so to show his team that he was not all powerful.

STAY BACK TIDAL FLOW!

GRAVY IN VIKING GRAVY BOAT

TRAY OF FOOD ARROWED, FLOATING AWAY ON THE TIDE:
(ROASTED HEART STUFFED WITH BACON AND LEEKS, BASTED WITH HONEY, AND SERVED WITH A GLASS OF MEAD)

(Colour in King Canute on the opposite page and give him any words you like. You can draw your own plate of food.)

*King Canute (King Cnut) was King of England, Denmark and Norway …united as the North Sea Empire.*

# EVEN MORE ANGLO-SAXONS AND DANES !

Harold Number one
Was Canute's illegitimate son
Had a short three year reign
Then came the official heir of Canute
Called Harthacanute
And the Danes were in charge again

Edward the Confessor
Was not an aggressor
And became England's first patron Saint
He promised William the throne
But when he was gone
Harold was elected with no restraint

William the Conqueror
Was no idle ponderer
When invading England's shore
"Holy Cross!" Harold's cry
But arrow in his eye*
Meant he lost the war

*Disputed
(Illustration based loosely on the Bayeux Tapestry
You can add a load of flying arrows if you like)

* The sea is very cold

# NORMANS AND PLANTAGENETS
# 1066-1485

Normans and Plantagenets
Beat all the pundits bets
And reigned for four hundred years
Even today
It's true to say
They're our rulers' distant forebears*

Norman, Plantagenet,
Lancastrians and Yorkist
Killed opposition of any who resist

## NORMANS

There was William One and William the Second
Henry One and Stephen

Cousin Matilda fought Stevie
In the Anarchy
She stopped fighting
When Stephen agreed
That her son Henry would be the one to succeed

## PLANTAGENETS

Henry the Second was a strong king
Most of France he would bring
In line with the England throne
He argued with Thomas Becket
Henry's men did not check it
And cut Becket to the bone

Richard the Lionheart had a ten year reign
But spent most of his time in lands foreign
He led the Third Crusade
Though strong and handsome
He was captured, held for ransom
A very large sum was paid.

*Charles III is a direct descendant of William the Conqueror but so, statistically, are most of the inhabitants of Western Europe.*

# PLANTAGENETS CONTINUED

John ruled badly
Louis came from France
Ruled for maybe five months
Led the barons a merry dance

The legends of this time
Put Robin Hood in the rhyme
He lived in the glen
With his merry men
Robbed the rich to pay the poor
Not once but again and a-gen *

Robin Hood in the forest stood
Fired an arrow into the sky
It hovered for ages
Then went back four pages
And hit Harold right in the eye

John died
No-one cried

His elder son was legitimate heir
So Henry the Third followed John
Next Edward the First came along
And defeated the Welsh princes
Made his son Prince of Wales
Hammered the Scots
And at his name Scotland winces.

\* ROBIN HOOD IS A DISPUTED LEGEND

*From left to right: Little John, Robin Hood, at the back the Sheriff of Nottingham, at the front Friar Tuck and behind him (with an apple on his head) William Tell's son (from a different book!). Have a look for a wayward arrow!*

# PLANTAGENETS CONTINUED

Edward the second was murdered in Berkeley
Edward the third viewed Mortimer darkly
For having arranged the crimes
Edward Three
Ruled successfully
Though the Black Death made it dark times

Richard the second
Certainly reckoned
He'd got the better of Wat Tyler
Henry the Fourth*
Returned from exile, but of course
He was not a four minute miler**.

English was Henry's
Native tongue
Whereas French had been
The Royal scene
Since Norman Conquest was
On England sprung

(* First king from the House of Lancaster: a cadet branch of the house of Plantagenet)

(**The first sub-four minute mile was run by Roger Bannister 1954)

Henry V is remembered for Agincourt
When English archers put the French on the floor
Henries Vee and Vee One
Then the Yorkists won*
Followed by Edwards four and five
The latter in the Tower was not very long alive

Richard the Third's
Vision was blurred
His shape all twisted and weird
Princes in tower
Undermined Richard's power
So he had them disappeared**

(* The House of York was also a cadet branch of the house of Plantagenet)

(**Or was it Henry VII who did the dirty deeds? History is written by the winners because the losers are not usually in a position to do any writing.)

(Have a go at putting a little colour in the Tower of London and perhaps put your own words in the speech bubbles)

# THE TUDORS
## 1485-1603

Henry Tudor
Thought Richard a deluder
And the red rose was Henry's trade mark
At Bosworth Field
He made the white rose yield
They buried Richard in a car park*

*(\* The remains of Richard III were indeed found underneath a car park in Leicester but were originally buried in a friary church)*

Henry the Eighth
Was defender of the faith
Until he wanted divorce.**
Then in a Protestant lurch
He set up the Church
And removed his wives by force

"Divorced, beheaded, died
Divorced, beheaded, survived"

The ancient rhyme of the wives
Is not quite right
'Cos number four was annulled
And she lived the longest
Her senses un-dulled

*(\*\*See the end of the book for the names of the wives)*

*After Hans Holbein the Younger: portrait of Henry VIII.*

*Well, certainly not before him.
Holbein's painting was a long time ago. The newest one will be yours when you colour it in!*

# TUDORS CONTINUED

Edward the Sixth was Henry's only son
Six years then his reign was done

Lady Jane Grey
Lasted just six days

Of Bloody Mary
Protestants be wary
She killed in many ways
Now we've learned
Hundreds burned
It was a very bad phase.

Elizabeth the First
Had a terrible thirst
And refused to marry a man*
The Spanish tried harder
By sending Armada
But Drake spoiled their plan

*Some people say she secretly married and had children*

*Elizabeth's words "I have the heart …." are a famous quote. The reply is not!*

# STUARTS
## 1603-1714

From the far north came
England's first James
In Scotland he was James the Sixth
The first of our Stuarts
By golly he knew it
And believed in divine right of Kings

"Remember, remember
The fifth of November
Gunpowder , treason and plot.
I see no reason
Why gunpowder treason
Should ever be forgot"*

*Old Nursery Rhyme*
On the 5th November 1605 Guy Fawkes was caught with some 40 barrels of gunpowder in the catacombs under the House of Lords. He confessed that he was intending to blow up parliament when the king and all the lords were present.

## STUARTS CONTINUED

Charlie the First's
Blood vessels burst
As they chopped his head clean off
Next Cromwell severe,
When he died England cheered
The return of a Royal Toff

Charlie the Second's
Restoration beckoned
The reign of a popular King
Nearly twenty-five years
Of plague, fire and tears
But no official offspring

James number two
Tried to be true
To Roman Catholicism
Daughter Mary demurred
She and William preferred
To maintain the Protestant schism

Anne was a Stuart
But she went and blew it
By having no surviving child
Whilst James the pretender*
When out on a bender
'Cos his comeback plans went wild

*James the Old Pretender, son of James II, claimed the throne of England as James III but had only a few supporters and failed in his attempts to invade England.

## STUART PRETENDERS

"Speed, bonnie boat, like a bird on the wing.
Onward, the sailors cry!
Carry the lad that's born to be King
Over the sea to Skye."

"Loud the winds howls, loud the waves roar,
Thunderclaps rend the air.
Baffled our foes stand on the shore.
Follow they will not dare."*

* *Skye Boat Song: Late 19th century adaptation of a Gaelic song by William Ross c. 1782*

Bonnie Prince Charlie, son of James the Old Pretender, failed with his uprising in 1745 and escaped, dressed as a woman, with the help of Flora MacDonald.

# STUART PRETENDERS
## CONTINUED

Bonnie Prince Charlie
Hid in the barley
Dressed like a serving wench
So despite his good hair
With no legitimate heir
Cardinal Henry took substitute's bench*

*Why not paint or colour Bonnie Prince Charlie* and add your own sticks of barley?*

*Bonnie Prince Charlie was also known as the Young Pretender.*

\* Cardinal Henry was Bonnie Prince Charlie's younger brother and was the cardinal in charge of St Peter's in Rome. To the Jacobites—supporters of Stuart claims to the British throne—he was known as King Henry IX of Great Britain for the last 19 years of his life.

# HANOVERIANS

### 1714-1837

The Georges from Hanover
Came right over
To take up the English crown
Four Georges then Willie
All somewhat silly
And in some ways let the side down

I'll give you e.g
Mad George three
Who lost the colonies
Or George number four
Who barred his Queen from the door
Of coronation jollities

"Georgie Porgie, pudding and pie,
Kissed the girls and made them cry,
When the girls came out to play,
Georgie Porgie ran away."*

(* Old nursery rhyme about George IV)

Sorry about George III's belly. I wanted him to look suitably mad. He probably was not that fat.

George IV, on the other hand, was famously obese.

After James Gillray's Cartoon of G4

# SAXE-COBURG-GOTHA AND WINDSOR
## 1837-PRESENT

Queen Victoria seemed stuffy
Liked furniture fluffy
But married a handsome Prince
The numerous descendants
Were never repentant
And would not take anti-war hints

Edward number Seven's
Reign felt like heaven
Compared with George number Five
For World War One
Against cousin Kaiser Wilhelm was done
You were lucky to come out alive

Edward the Eighth
Was actually the eleventh
King Edward of olde England *
Abdicated the throne
With an audible groan
Lived in France but never in Finland

*Don't forget Edward the Elder, Edward the Martyr and Edward the Confessor all of whom came before Edward the First.

*Although Queen Victoria usually wore black you can colour her in bright colours if you'd like to cheer her up.
You could even turn her scowl into a smile!*

# HOUSE OF WINDSOR

George Six had a stutter
But some heard him mutter
"I wish my brother was still busy k k kinging.
Although I'm no strutter
If I eat brandy butter
I'm sure I'd have more fun from s s singing."

Elizabeth Two
Knew what to do
To maintain the monarchy's reign
She was no fool
"One does nothing!" her rule
Husband Philip was sparky, sarky and sane.

*Mr Ed was a talking horse in an American sitcom. Edward VIII was Elizabeth II's uncle who abdicated after less than a year on the throne and became the Duke of Windsor.*

## HOUSE OF WINDSOR CONTINUED

Now we've reached undeterred
Charles the Third
And his Queen is called Camilla
Cigarettes* were her scene
But busy Charlie has been
Building terraces and semi-detached villas

*(\*To her credit she gave up smoking in 2001 much to Charles' delight. Poundbury has now been passed on to Prince William, the new Duke of Cornwall)*

I've missed quite a few
Like the amazing ado
Of King John and the Magna Carta
Or the One Hundred Years War
And there is much, much more
I could go on pro rata, pro rata

*Colour Charles in and give him the last word by putting something in his speech bubble!*

# LIST OF RULERS OF OLDE ENGLAND*

## SAXON KINGS

EGBERT 827 – 839

AETHELWULF 839 – 858

AETHELBALD 858 – 860

AETHELBERT 860 – 866

AETHELRED I 866 – 871

ALFRED THE GREAT 871-899

EDWARD (The Elder) 899 – 924

ATHELSTAN 924 – 939

EDMUND 939 – 946

EADRED 946 – 955

EADWIG 955 – 959,

EDGAR 959 – 975

EDWARD THE MARTYR 975 – 978.

AETHELRED II THE UNREADY 978- 1013,1014-1016

## DANISH and SAXON KINGS

Danish: SWEYN from Christmas Day 1013   (For 5 weeks)

Saxons: AETHELRED II  returned after Sweyn died.

EDMUND II IRONSIDE 1016 – 1016

Danish:  CANUTE (CNUT THE GREAT)1016 – 1035

HAROLD I 1035 – 1040

HARTHACANUTE 1040 – 1042

Saxon: EDWARD THE CONFESSOR 1042-1066

HAROLD II 1066

## NORMAN KINGS

WILLIAM I (The Conqueror) 1066- 1087
WILLIAM II (Rufus) 1087-1100
HENRY I 1100-1135
STEPHEN 1135-1154
(Plus MATILDA 1139-1148 during the Anarchy)

## PLANTAGENET KINGS

HENRY II 1154-1189

RICHARD I (The Lionheart) 1189 – 1199

JOHN 1199 -1216

LOUIS 1216

HENRY III 1216 -1272

*Monarchs of England and Wales*

EDWARD I 1272 – 1307
EDWARD II 1307 – deposed 1327
EDWARD III 1327 – 1377
RICHARD II 1377 – deposed 1399

## HOUSE OF LANCASTER

HENRY IV 1399 – 1413
HENRY V 1413 – 1422
HENRY VI 1422 – deposed 1461
Beginning of the Wars of the Roses

* Adapted from: English Kings https://www.historic-uk.com/HistoryUK/KingsQueensofBritain/

## HOUSE OF YORK

EDWARD IV 1461- 1483
EDWARD V 1483 – 1483
RICHARD III 1483 – 1485

End of the Wars of the Roses

## THE TUDORS

HENRY VII 1485 – 1509

*Monarchs of England, Wales and Ireland*

HENRY VIII 1509 – 1547*
EDWARD VI 1547 – 1553
LADY JANE GREY 1553
MARY I (Bloody Mary) 1553 – 1558
ELIZABETH I 1558-1603

*British Monarchs*

## THE STUARTS

JAMES I and VI of Scotland 1603 -1625
CHARLES 1 1625 – 1649

English Civil War

## THE COMMONWEALTH declared May 19th 1649

OLIVER CROMWELL, Lord Protector 1653 – 1658
RICHARD CROMWELL, Lord Protector 1658 – 1659

*Wives of Henry VIII*
- Catherine of Aragon: Divorced by Church of England
- Anne Boleyn: Beheaded
- Jane Seymour: Died 12 days after giving birth
- Anne of Cleves: Annulled and outlived all the other wives
- Catherine Howard: Beheaded
- Catherine Parr: Outlived Henry VIII by 18 months

## THE RESTORATION of MONARCHY

CHARLES II 1660 – 1685
JAMES II and VII of Scotland 1685 – 1688
WILLIAM III 1689 – 1702 and MARY II 1689 – 1694
ANNE 1702 – 1714

## THE HANOVERIANS

GEORGE I 1714 -1727
GEORGE II 1727 – 1760
GEORGE III 1760 – 1820
GEORGE IV 1820 – 1830
WILLIAM IV 1830 – 1837
VICTORIA 1837 – 1901

## HOUSE OF SAXE-COBURG AND GOTHA

EDWARD VII 1901 – 1910

## HOUSE OF WINDSOR

Name changed in 1917

GEORGE V 1910 – 1936
EDWARD VIII June 1936 – abdicated December 1936
GEORGE VI 1936 – 1952
ELIZABETH II 1952 – 2022
CHARLES III 2022 –

Also from Clinical Press:

**The British Time Scale:**
***Half a million years illustrated***
by Gary James
*Rated ***** Brilliant*

In a conveniently portable folded book format, the timescale will also expand into a wall chart of 2 metres in length and includes 25 maps. In full colour.
ISBN: 1 85457 043 9